DATE DUE		

The Urbana Free Library

To renew: call 217-367-4057
or go to "*urbanafreelibrary.org*"
and select "Renew/Request Items"

The Truth About TROLLS

by Thomas Kingsley Troupe

illustrated by Bridget Starr Taylor

PICTURE WINDOW BOOKS

a capstone imprint

Thanks to our advisers for their expertise, research, and advice:

Elizabeth Tucker, Ph.D., Professor of English
Binghamton University, Binghamton, New York

Terry Flaherty, Ph.D., Professor of English
Minnesota State University, Mankato

Editors: Shelly Lyons and Jennifer Besel
Designer: Lori Bye
Art Director: Nathan Gassman
Production Specialist: Jane Klenk
The illustrations in this book were created with colored chalk, pastel, and acrylic wash.

Picture Window Books
151 Good Counsel Drive
P.O. Box 669
Mankato, MN 56002-0669
877-845-8392
www.capstonepub.com

All books published by Picture Window Books
are manufactured with paper containing at least
10 percent post-consumer waste.

Library of Congress Cataloging-in-Publication Data
Troupe, Thomas Kingsley.
The truth about trolls / written by Thomas Kingsley Troupe ;
illustrated by Bridget Starr Taylor.
p. cm. — (Fairy-tale superstars)
Includes index
ISBN 978-1-4048-5984-5 (library binding)
1. Trolls—Juvenile literature. I. Taylor, Bridget Starr,
1959- ill. II. Title.
GR555.T76 2010
398.21—dc22   2009030067

Printed in the United States of America in North Mankato, Minnesota.
092010   005942R

Beware of Trolls!

Trolls might seem hairy and scary, but are they real? Of course not! Trolls are make-believe creatures from very old stories.

History of Trolls

Trolls are imaginary monsters from Norwegian, Swedish, and Danish legends. In many stories, they are mean characters. But heroes always outsmart or win battles against the tricky trolls!

Where did trolls come from? One myth tells us that the first troll sprang from the feet of a giant named Ymir.

What Do Trolls Look Like?

Storybook trolls are strange-looking creatures. They have long, strong arms and big hands. Their teeth are sharp and scary. They have big noses and large ears. Many trolls have long, shaggy hair that covers their faces. Their noses poke out from behind the long hair.

Trolls also have large heads, but their brains are small. They are very easy to trick!

In legends, some trolls seem as tall as trees. Some are even as big as a mountain! The ground rumbles when they walk. Their shouts echo across the land.

shaggy hair

huge ears

large nose

dirt-covered foot

Trolls almost always look strange and messy.
They are covered with dirt and hate to take baths.
Trees sometimes grow out of their heads and feet!

Troll Behavior

Trolls like to eat, but they hate to cook. Many trolls frighten people into giving them meals. In some stories, trolls steal human babies and leave troll babies behind! Trolls may try to eat children or animals.

Some trolls are greedy. They collect gold and riches. In some tales, children fool the monsters and escape with treasure.

Where Do Trolls Live?

Trolls are too big to live in houses. Most live outdoors in dark, thick woods. Some trolls live inside old, hollow trees.

A few trolls live in mountain caves. Dark places are perfect for them. They like to hide under rocks and sleep the day away.

Storybook trolls often live under bridges. The bridges give the trolls shade and keep them hidden.

When these trolls hear people pass by, they yell horrible words. Sometimes they trap people who try to cross their bridges.

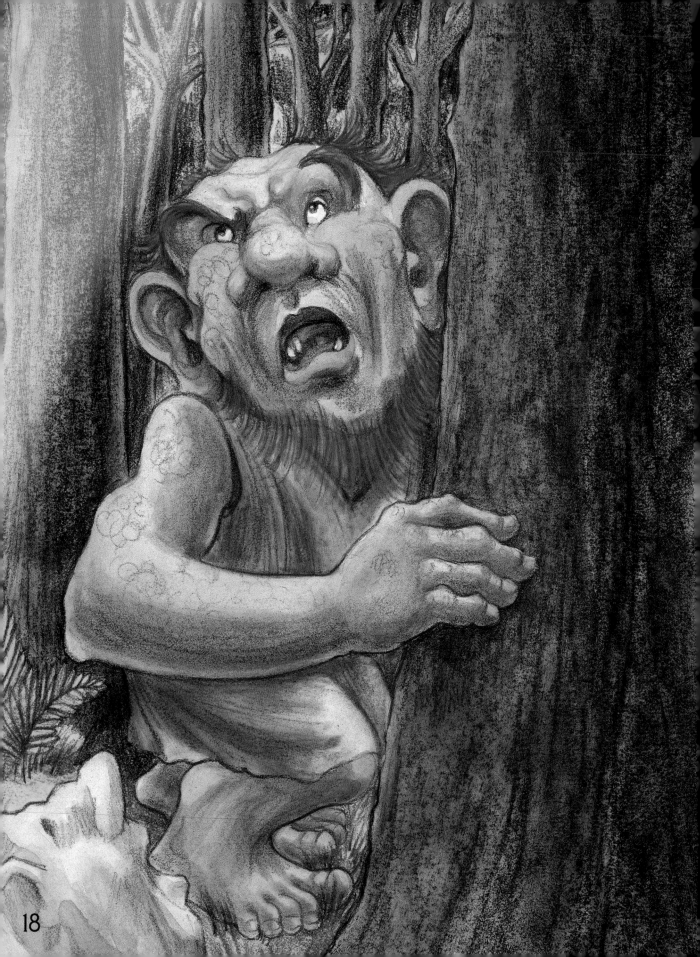

Trolls live in dark places to avoid sunlight. When sunlight touches a troll, the troll turns into a stone. A large rock in the forest may have once been a troll!

Troll Tales

Tales of trolls have been told for hundreds of years. Troll stories are still popular today.

One famous troll tale is *The Three Billy Goats Gruff*. Three goats meet a troll who lives under a bridge. The goats outsmart the troll. They cross the bridge to get to the tasty grass on the other side.

Butterball is a scary tale about a boy who looks tasty to an old troll woman. The troll tricks Butterball into climbing into a sack three different times.

Each time, Butterball escapes being cooked into a stew. Instead, he steals the troll's gold and becomes a rich man.

Troll Sightings

Trolls turn up in the strangest places. Some people think they see trolls in giant rocks and twisted trees.

In Scandinavia, there are many troll statues. The biggest statue is the Senja Troll in Norway. It's almost 59 feet (18 meters) tall. It weighs more than 275,000 pounds (125,000 kilograms)!

In the United States, a giant troll statue hides under the Aurora Bridge in Seattle, Washington. It's called the Freemont Troll. The troll holds a small car in its huge hand.

Mount Horeb, Wisconsin, is known as the "Troll Capital of the World." Mount Horeb's main street is called "The Trollway." It is lined with troll statues. Many shops and restaurants there have trolls too.

Trolls Today

Today, make-believe trolls are not all big, ugly, and scary. Some troll toys are cute, with brightly colored hair.

Scary or not, these mythical creatures are just pretend. Still, it's fun to imagine they are real—as long as they stay deep in the woods!

Fun Facts About Trolls

- According to legend, some female trolls were beautiful enough to make human men fall in love with them.

- Storytellers say trolls can have more than one head. Some of them have as many as 12! Sadly, they get headaches from shouting at each other all the time.

- In many troll tales, children who are naughty or foolish become smart enough to trick trolls.

- In the past, some people often blamed their poor luck on trolls.

- Not all trolls are huge. Some trolls from Swedish and Danish tales are smaller. Unlike the Norwegian trolls, they are more bothersome than mean.

Glossary

greedy—selfishly wanting something, such as money or treasure

imagine—to picture something in your mind

legend—a story handed down from earlier times

myth—a make-believe story

mythical—make-believe or imaginary

outsmart—to trick someone

Scandinavia—the area of land that includes the countries of Norway, Sweden, and Denmark

shaggy—untidy or messy

Index

To Learn More

More Books to Read

Asbjørnsen, Peter Christen. *The Three Billy Goats Gruff.* New York: Clarion, 2006.

Asbjørnsen, Peter Christen. *The Troll with No Heart in His Body and Other Tales of Trolls from Norway: Retold by Lise Lunge-Larsen.* Boston: Houghton Mifflin, 1999.

D'Aulaire, Ingri, and Edgar Parin d'Aulaire. *D'Aulaires' Book of Trolls.* New York: New York Review of Books, 2006.

Internet Sites

FactHound offers a safe, fun way to find Internet sites related to this book. All of the sites on FactHound have been researched by our staff.

Here's all you do:

Visit *www.facthound.com*

FactHound will fetch the best sites for you!

Look for all the books in the Fairy-Tale Superstars series:

The Truth About Dragons
The Truth About Fairies

The Truth About Princesses
The Truth About Trolls